SCHOLASTIC

Science
Graphic Organizers
& Mini-Lessons

by Maria L. Chang

NEW YORK • TORONTO • LONDON • AUCKLAND • SYDNEY
MEXICO CITY • NEW DELHI • HONG KONG • BUENOS AIRES

Teaching *Resources*

Dedication

To Zachary and Jeremy,
you make my life complete

Cover design by Maria Lilja
Interior design by Jeffrey Dorman
Illustrations by Dave Clegg

ISBN 0-439-54896-9
Copyright © 2006 by Maria L. Chang

4 5 6 7 8 9 10   40   12 11 10 09

Contents

Introduction

Science and graphic organizers are natural partners in teaching and learning. Science encompasses an immense amount of content knowledge that extends across several disciplines. Graphic organizers, on the other hand, offer frameworks to help students identify important information, outline knowledge, recognize relationships—in other words, make sense of all this information. Creating visual and spatial representations of science information provides students with a type of scaffolding that helps them grow into independent learners. The graphic organizers in this book are designed to help students build important process skills, understand key concepts, and meet the science standards.

What Is a Graphic Organizer?

A graphic organizer is a visual and graphic representation of relationships among ideas and concepts. This instructional tool comes in a variety of formats—from loose webs to structured grids—that help students process information they've gathered and organize their ideas. We generally design graphic organizers to follow one of four patterns of knowledge: hierarchical, conceptual, sequential, and cyclical (Bromley et al., 1995).

Hierarchical organizers use principles of rank and order to help students break down a concept. For example, the "Steps of the Scientific Method" organizer (page 8) offers a hierarchical structure that helps students move systematically through the stages of conducting an experiment—from developing a research question to devising a foolproof procedure, to formulating a conclusion based on results.

Conceptual organizers, such as webs, provide a format for enumerating the attributes of the main topic or idea. The nonlinear, open-ended structure assists students in generating ideas for a topic. The "Word Connections" organizer (page 26) is an example of a conceptual organizer characterized by a central space for recording an important science concept and radiating spaces in which students can list related vocabulary words and connect them to more familiar words.

Sequential organizers are used to show time-order relationships. Often linear in format, they can help students link causes and effects, sort chronological events, and identify problem-solution relationships. A good example of this format is the "Series of Events" organizer (page 30) in which students write the sequence of events that occur in a particular process, such as digestion or the formation of a volcano.

Cyclical organizers are used to show an ordered series of events that are part of a repeating pattern. The circular structure of these graphic organizers helps students present, in order, each element in a series, cycle, or succession. For example, the circular pattern in "Follow the Cycle" organizer (page 28) offers a way to show the continuous sequence of steps in an organism's life cycle.

Why Use Graphic Organizers?

Graphic organizers make teaching and learning more rewarding. Visually appealing and accessible to both struggling and advanced students, graphic organizers help students to:

- connect prior knowledge to new information (Guastello, 2000);
- integrate language and thinking in an organized format (Bromley et al., 1995);
- increase comprehension and retention of text (Boyle & Weishaar, 1997; Chang, K. et al, 2002; Moore & Readence, 1984);
- organize writing (Ellis, 1994);
- engage in mid- to high levels of thinking along Bloom's Taxonomy (application, analysis, evaluation, and synthesis) (Dodge, 2005).

How Are the Organizers Arranged in This Book?

The 20 graphic organizers in this book are grouped in two sections: Process Skills and Science Concepts. In the first section, the organizers focus on key process skills in science, such as making observations, collecting data, comparing and contrasting, classifying, and more. The organizers in the second section are designed to assist students as they navigate the tremendous amount of content in science, helping them analyze and visually organize information.

Using the Lessons and Graphic Organizers in This Book

The organizers can be used flexibly for a variety of learning situations for students in grades 4–6: whole class, small groups, and individuals. Use them as motivational graphic aids to teach and practice skills and concepts or use them as resources to support students in reading, writing, and researching.

One factor influencing the effectiveness of graphic organizers is the instructional context in which they are used. Studies suggest that to maximize the impact of graphic organizers on student learning, teachers need to state the purpose for using the organizer, model how to use it, and provide students with multiple opportunities for guided and independent practice and feedback.

(National Center on Accessing the General Curriculum, 2002)

Each lesson includes a skills focus, a statement of purpose, teaching suggestions, a student sample, and a reproducible graphic organizer.

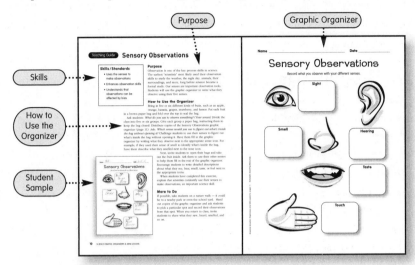

You can implement the organizers in any of the following ways:
- Draw the organizer on the board or on chart paper.
- Use the organizer as a template for an overhead transparency.
- Reproduce multiple copies of the organizer to pass out to students during class work.
- Have copies of the organizer available for students to use while reading and working independently.

For whole-class instruction, use the lessons and the graphic organizers to model how to organize information visually. Invite students to offer ideas and suggest where this information would go in the organizer; this helps build background for their own independent or small-group work.

For small-group instruction, use the lessons and graphic organizers to provide students with the opportunity to work and learn cooperatively. When students are familiar with the format and purpose of an organizer, you can adapt it for use as a game or group activity. As students build background and brainstorm together, their learning is enriched by one another's experiences.

For independent learning, use the graphic organizers to keep students engaged and focused on learning objectives. Once you've demonstrated how to complete the organizer, provide students with copies of the reproducible so they may complete their own during independent work time.

Use the lessons and graphic organizers in this book to help make science an exciting and successful part of your students' learning experience.

Steps of the Scientific Method

Skills/Standards

- Understands the nature of scientific inquiry

- Understands the scientific method

- Plans and conducts simple investigations

Purpose

Doing scientific research is not just some random activity that scientists engage in when they want to find out about something. When conducting research or experiments, scientists often use a step-by-step process called the *scientific method*. Students need to follow this same process to conduct experiments, whether for the lab or a science fair.

How to Use the Organizer

Ask students: *When scientists want to find out something, like how or why something works, what do they do? (They conduct an experiment.)* Explain to students that when scientists conduct experiments, they follow a step-by-step process called the *scientific method*. Students are expected to follow the same steps when conducting an experiment in the lab or for a science fair. Distribute copies of the Steps of the Scientific Method graphic organizer (page 9) and go over the different steps with students.

Explain that the first step of the scientific method is to ask a *research question*; for example, which brand of bubble gum blows the biggest bubble? The next step is to state a *hypothesis*, or an educated guess about the research question. This is usually based on prior knowledge or research conducted to find out what is already known about the topic. Next comes the *procedure,* a step-by-step plan for conducting the experiment. A detailed procedure includes a list of *materials* and their amounts, as well as specific directions for conducting the experiment. Detailed directions allow someone else to repeat the experiment exactly the way it was done. After writing the procedure, it's time to conduct the actual experiment and collect *data*. Scientists show their data using graphs, charts, or tables. Finally, based on these results, they draw a *conclusion*—the answer to their research question.

Have students use this graphic organizer whenever they're conducting experiments to ensure they follow the steps of the scientific method correctly.

Name Joanna   Date 12/12

Steps of the Scientific Method

Use this graphic organizer to plan your science experiment.

Research Question
Which brand of battery lasts longest?

Hypothesis
Brand C will last the longest.

Materials
3 different brands of AA batteries
6 strips of aluminum foil
3 flashlight bulbs
3 clothespins   tape
3 rubber bands

Procedure
Set up each battery as follows: Wrap a rubber band around the battery lengthwise. Slip one end of a foil strip to the top of the battery under the rubber band. Wrap one end of another foil strip around the bulb's base. Use the clothespin to hold the strip and bulb in place. Tape the other end of the strip to the bottom of the bulb. When all three batteries have been set up, connect each battery's 2 foil strips to the light bulb. Use a time to see how long each battery lasts.

Data
Brand A lasted 37 minutes.
Brand B lasted 25 minutes.
Brand C lasted 44 minutes.

Conclusion
Brand C lasted longest.

Steps of the Scientific Method

Use this graphic organizer to plan your science experiment.

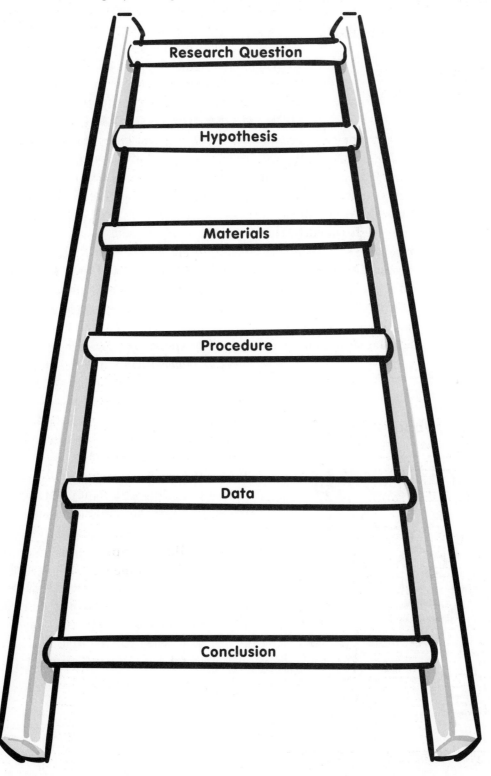

Research Question

Hypothesis

Materials

Procedure

Data

Conclusion

Sensory Observations

Skills/Standards

- Uses the senses to make observations

- Enhances observation skills

- Understands that observations can be affected by bias

Purpose

Observation is one of the key process skills in science. The earliest "scientists" most likely used their observation skills to study the weather, the night sky, animals, their surroundings, and more, long before science became a formal study. Our senses are important observation tools. Students will use the graphic organizer to write what they observe using their five senses.

How to Use the Organizer

Bring in five or six different kinds of fruits, such as an apple, orange, banana, grapes, strawberry, and lemon. Put each fruit in a brown paper bag and fold over the top to seal the bag.

Ask students: *What do you use to observe something? (Your senses)* Divide the class into five or six groups. Give each group a paper bag, instructing them to keep the bag closed. Distribute copies of the Sensory Observations graphic organizer (page 11). Ask: *Which senses would you use to figure out what's inside the bag without opening it?* Challenge students to use their senses to figure out what's inside the bag without opening it. Have them fill in the graphic organizer by writing what they observe next to the appropriate sense icon. For example, if they used their sense of smell to identify what's inside the bag, have them describe what they smelled next to the nose icon.

Next, invite students to open their bags and take out the fruit inside. Ask them to use their other senses to help them fill in the rest of the graphic organizer. Encourage students to write detailed descriptions about what they see, hear, smell, taste, or feel next to the appropriate icons.

When students have completed this exercise, explain that scientists constantly use their senses to make observations, an important science skill.

More to Do

If possible, take students on a nature walk — it could be to a nearby park or even the school yard. Hand out copies of the graphic organizer and ask students to pick a particular spot and record their observations from that spot. When you return to class, invite students to share what they saw, heard, smelled, and so on.

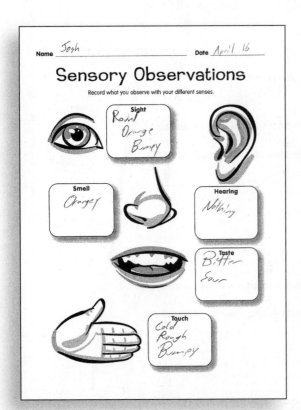

Sensory Observations

Record what you observe with your different senses.

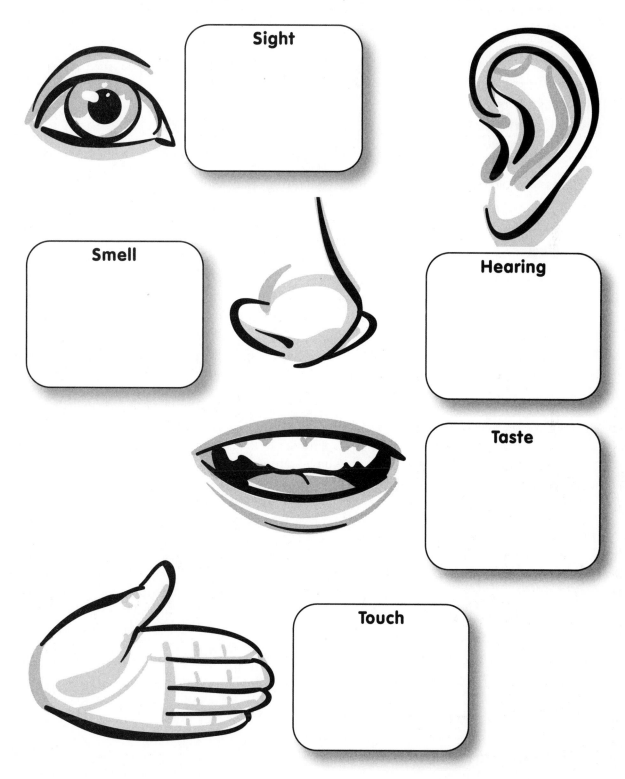

Sight

Smell

Hearing

Taste

Touch

Research Notes

Skills / Standards

- Understands the nature of scientific knowledge

- Understands the nature of scientific inquiry

- Knows that scientific investigations involve asking and answering questions and comparing the answer to what scientists already know

- Gathers and uses information for research purposes

- Collects and organizes information from multiple sources

Purpose

Whether conducting research for a science report or for a project, students will benefit from this graphic organizer that helps them collect and organize the information they need. Students can use this graphic organizer in conjunction with "Steps of the Scientific Method" (page 8) when they conduct research to find existing information about their research question.

How to Use the Organizer

Distribute copies of the Research Notes graphic organizer (page 13) to students. Have students use this graphic organizer to help them collect and organize information for their research, as well as to keep track of their sources.

Discuss some basics of research note-taking with students. To help focus their research, students should first decide on a topic or research question. Have students record their topic or research question at the top of the page. Next, have students think about where they can find the information they need; for example, a textbook, newspaper or magazine article, or Web site. Ask them to scan through each source to see if it contains relevant information. When they've identified a likely source, have students write its name or title on the appropriate space on an index card.

Teach students how to identify important ideas from a source, making sure that the information is pertinent to their research question. Have them jot down all their notes from the same source on one index card. Emphasize that they should paraphrase and/or summarize main ideas rather than copy down complete sentences. Not only does this make it easier to fit copy into the limited recording space, it also reduces the risk of plagiarism. Distribute additional copies of the graphic organizer to students as needed.

When students are confident that they have collected enough information about their topic or research question, have them synthesize their notes to write their report or hypothesis.

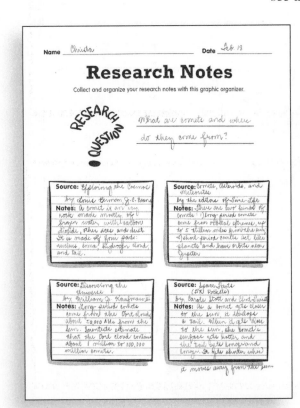

Research Notes

Collect and organize your research notes with this graphic organizer.

RESEARCH QUESTION _____
_____

Source: _____

Notes: _____

Source: _____

Notes: _____

Source: _____

Notes: _____

Source: _____

Notes: _____

Data Collector

Skills/Standards

- Uses appropriate tools and simple equipment to gather, analyze, and interpret scientific data

- Identifies independent and dependent variables

- Recognizes that an experiment must be repeated many times and yield consistent results before the results are accepted as correct

- Organizes and interprets data

Purpose

When conducting experiments, scientists (and students) are often bombarded with various data or quantifiable results from their experiments. While grabbing a random piece of scrap paper to jot down numbers is often tempting, it makes more sense to record all these data on a table. This way, the data is organized and easier to interpret later on. This graphic organizer provides a place for students to record their data from experiments.

How to Use the Organizer

Explain to students that an important part of conducting an experiment is collecting data. First, they need to be aware of the different variables in the experiment. Ask: *What is a variable? (An element or characteristic in an experiment that changes)* Explain that an experiment often has two kinds of variables—an *independent variable* (the variable you change on purpose) and a *dependent variable* (the variable that changes in response to a change in the independent variable). For example, if you're conducting an experiment to find out which brand of ice cream melts the fastest, the independent variable is the brand of ice cream and the dependent variable is the melting time.

Display a transparency copy of the Data Collector graphic organizer (page 15) on the overhead projector. Explain to students that when collecting data, they should list the independent variable on one side of the chart and record the changes in the dependent variable next to it. On the transparency, label that top row of the first column *Ice Cream Brand*, then list the following in that column: *Brand A*, *Brand B*, and *Brand C*. On the top row of the next column, write *Melting Time (in minutes)*. Point out the different "Trial" columns to students. Explain that they should do repeated trials when doing an experiment to verify results, and they should take the average when graphing results.

Distribute copies of the graphic organizer to students and have them use it to record their data when conducting an experiment.

Name *Christa*   Date *Vol. 5*

Data Collector

As you conduct your experiment, record the data you collect on this graphic organizer

Research Question: How does the amount of fat affect how much cheese stretches?				
Independent Variable: Fat content of cheese	**Dependent Variable:** Stretchability of cheese (in cm)			
	Trial 1	Trial 2	Trial 3	Average
0% fat cheese (no fat)	10	8	9	9
2% fat cheese (low fat)	14	16	14	14.7
4% fat cheese (regular)	22	19	19	20

What type of graph best shows your data? Circle one:
line graph   bar graph   circle graph   other

Name _____

Date _____

Data Collector

As you conduct your experiment, record the data you collect on this graphic organizer.

Research Question:

Independent Variable:

Dependent Variable:

	Trial 1	Trial 2	Trial 3	Average

What type of graph best shows your data? Circle one:

line graph   bar graph   circle graph   other

Comparison Close-Up

Skills/Standards

- Identifies traits, characteristics, or attributes of objects

- Compares and contrasts two things

- Recognizes relationships between two things

Purpose

Using a Venn diagram, students can list characteristics or attributes of two (or more) things and notice how they are different and what they have in common. Science, in particular, offers many opportunities for students to compare different things using Venn diagrams. Students can use this graphic organizer for a wide variety of topics.

How to Use the Organizer

Distribute photocopies of the Comparison Close-Up graphic organizer (page 17) to students and display a transparency on the overhead projector. Explain that this type of graphic organizer is called a Venn diagram and that it's used to compare and contrast two different things.

For example, say you wanted to compare a shark with a dolphin. Write the word *shark* on the handle of one magnifying lens and the word *dolphin* on the other handle. Ask students: *What characteristics do sharks have that dolphins do not? (It is a fish, it breathes through gills, it has rows of sharp teeth, and so on.)* List students' answers in the "shark" lens. Next, ask students to name attributes of dolphins that are different from sharks. *(It is a mammal, it breathes air through its blowhole, it has small teeth, and so on.)* List responses in the "dolphin" lens. Finally, ask: *What do these two animals have in common? (They live in the ocean, eat fish, have similar-looking dorsal fins, and so on.)* Write these attributes on the overlapping area between the two lenses.

With students working individually or in pairs, have them pick two things or topics to compare and contrast using the organizer. (You may want to brainstorm ideas as a class, then let students choose what things to compare.) Encourage students to use prior knowledge and research new information about the things or topics they're comparing.

Name _____

Date _____

Comparison Close-Up

List characteristics of two things and identify what they have in common.

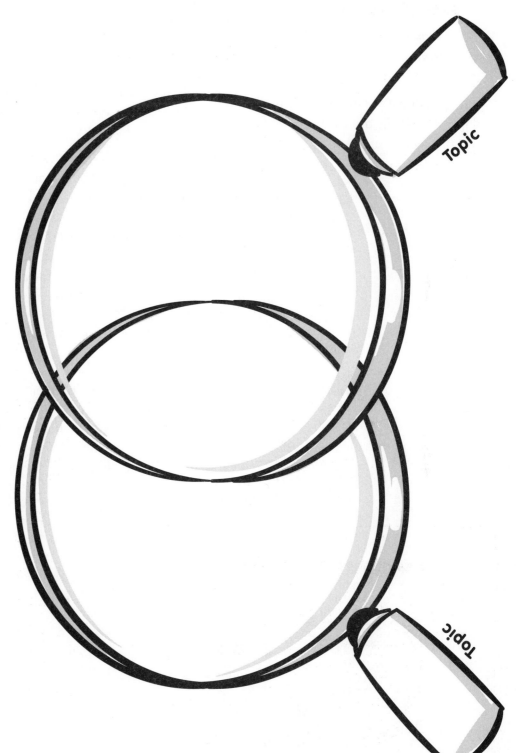

Topic

Topic

Mission Classification

Skills/Standards

- Identifies different ways in which living (and nonliving) things can be grouped

- Classifies things based on how they are alike

Purpose

To help make sense of the world around us, we often try to sort things into groups based on what they have in common. This process is called *classification*. Scientists have classified everything on earth as living or nonliving. Living things are classified further into plants, animals, fungi, protists (like paramecia and amoebas), and monerans (like bacteria). Animals are classified into vertebrates and invertebrates, and so on. This graphic organizer will help students classify various things.

How to Use the Organizer

List the following words on the board: *rock, cactus, book, computer, grass, fish, tree, river, chair, horse, cloud,* and *dinosaur.* Ask students to look at the list and decide how they might group the various things on the board. Give students a few minutes, then call on volunteers to sort everything on the list into two groups and to name those two groups. Accept reasonable responses until someone mentions "living and nonliving things." Ask another volunteer to come up to the board and circle everything on the list that is a living thing.

Display a transparency copy of the Mission Classification graphic organizer (page 19) on the overhead projector and write *living things* on the top space. Have students look at the circled words and ask them: *How can we further classify the living things on this list? (They can be classified as plants and animals.)* Write the words *plants* and *animals* in the boxes on the second level of the graphic organizer. Then have students fill in the next level of boxes with the things that belong to these two groups. *(Cactus, grass, and tree under "plants"; fish, horse, and dinosaur under "animals")*

Distribute copies of the graphic organizer to students and have them classify the nonliving things on the list using the graphic organizer. (The nonliving things can be further classified into natural and human-made.) Encourage students to use the graphic organizer to classify other things, like types of animals (e.g., mammals and reptiles), types of plants (e.g., those that make seeds and those that don't), and so on. Encourage students to add their own boxes to extend the graphic organizer if necessary.

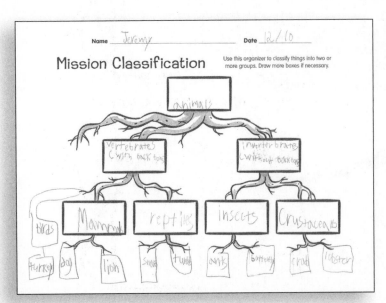

Mission Classification

Use this organizer to classify things into two or more groups. Draw more boxes if necessary.

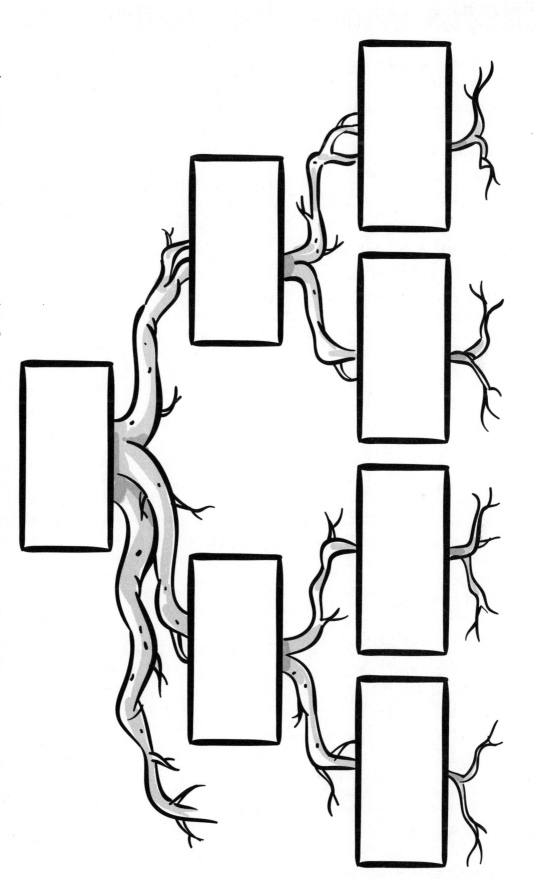

Cause-and-Effect Flow Chart

Skills/Standards

- Develops critical-thinking skills

- Understands cause-and-effect relationships

- Identifies causes for effects and vice-versa

- Understands cause-and-effect relationships

- Sequences a chain of events

Purpose

Many events in science (and in the world) often happen as a result of something else. The event that makes something happen is called the *cause*, and what happens as a result is the *effect*. Often the effect itself becomes a cause for something else. This new "effect," in turn, becomes the cause for something else again. The result is like a chain reaction, with one event triggering another event, which triggers another, and so on. This graphic organizer helps students recognize that everything happens for a reason and has consequences.

How to Use the Organizer

Make a transparency of the Cause-and-Effect Flow Chart graphic organizer (page 21) and display it on the overhead projector. Explain to students that this particular graphic organizer helps show that several events or phenomena in science are really a series of causes and effects. Take for example global warming. Ask students: *What do you think causes global warming? (Answers will vary, but could include burning of fossil fuels and cutting down trees.)*

On the transparency, write "Burning fossil fuels" in the top cup. Ask: *What happens when we burn fossil fuels? (Carbon dioxide is released into the air.)* In the second cup, write "CO_2 is released in the air." Explain that carbon dioxide is a type of greenhouse gas, which traps heat in our atmosphere. Write "Heat trapped in atmosphere" in the third cup. Ask students what should be in the next cup. *(Global warming)* Next, ask students: *What do you think is an effect of global warming? (Answers will vary, but could include change in weather patterns, rising sea levels, and harm to ocean life.)* Choose a reasonable answer to write in the last cup.

Point out that even though this graphic organizer allows for only five events, students could continue past the last cup (e.g., *What could be an effect of rising sea levels?*), or even go back before the event in the first cup (e.g., *Why are we burning fossil fuels?*). Distribute copies of the graphic organizer to students. Have them choose a topic that lends itself to this cause-and-effect flow chart. Encourage students to conduct research to find the causes and effects of their topic. Let them work individually, with partners, or in small groups.

Cause-and-Effect Flow Chart

Cause-and-Effect Flow Chart

Pick a science topic or event. List the causes and effects that stem from this event.

Topic: _____

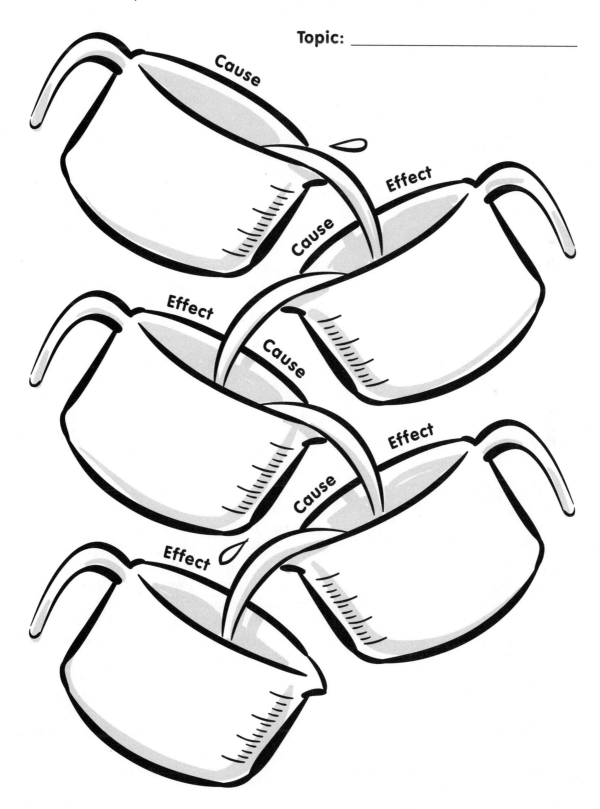

Branches of Science

Skills/Standards

- Understands the nature of scientific knowledge

- Defines science

- Describes the three main branches of science—life, earth, and physical sciences

- Explores various topics that are part of each branch

Purpose

Science is a very large body of knowledge that covers a wide range of topics. Using this graphic organizer, students will explore the different topics we study in science and gain a better understanding of the breadth of science.

How to Use the Organizer

Make a transparency of the Branches of Science graphic organizer (page 23), as well as photocopies for students. Ask students: *What is science? (A body of knowledge that deals with the physical world in general, based on observation and experimentation) What things do we learn about when we study science?* List students' responses on the board. When you have about a dozen or so answers, divide the class into small groups. Have them look at the list and find ways to categorize the different topics.

Display the transparency on the overhead projector. In the tree trunk, write the word *science*. Call on different groups to share how they categorized the list of topics on the board. Guide the discussion until students mention *life science, earth science,* or *physical science.* Write those words on each of the three branches coming from the trunk and explain to students that everything we study in science falls under these three main categories.

Distribute copies of the graphic organizer to students, and have them copy the words on the transparency. Working individually or in small groups, have students brainstorm topics (other than the ones already listed on the board) that are part of each branch of science. Have them fill in the upper branches of the tree with the topics they brainstormed.

More to Do

Encourage students to explore each branch of science more closely by having them write *life science, earth science,* or *physical science* on the main trunk. Challenge them to determine some of the discipline's main branches (for example, meteorology, astronomy, or paleontology for earth science) and topics that are part of each branch.

Branches of Science

Record a major area of science on the tree trunk.
Then list other topics that branch off this major area.

KWHL

Skills/Standards

- Understands the nature of scientific knowledge

- Knows that scientific investigations involve asking and answering a question and comparing the answer to what scientists already know about the world

- Activates prior knowledge about a topic

- Generates questions about a topic

- Conducts research to find answers to questions

Purpose

Prior to introducing a new topic, it's often a good idea to have students fill out a KWL chart (what students **know**, what they **want** to know, and what they **learned**). Using this chart, students can activate their prior knowledge about the topic and generate questions to guide their search for more information. As they conduct research to answer their questions, they can record what they've learned. The KWHL graphic organizer goes one step further by asking students to record **how** they might find the information they need. Using this graphic organizer will help students monitor and take responsibility for their own learning.

How to Use the Organizer

Decide on a new topic that you would like to introduce to students. Display a transparency copy of the KWHL graphic organizer (page 25) on the overhead projector and distribute photocopies to students. Write the topic above the chart and have students copy it down on their graphic organizers. Ask students: *What do you know about this topic?* List their responses in the first column of the chart under "K," making sure students copy along as you write. Then ask students what they want to know about the topic. Have them phrase their response in the form of a question. List their questions in the second column under "W."

Next, have students think about how they might go about finding answers to their questions. Ask: *What resources can we use when looking for information? (Encyclopedia, textbook, newspaper and magazine articles, the Internet)* For each question in the second column, ask students what might be a good source for an answer. Remind students that sometimes the answer could come from an expert or even from a scientific formula. List their responses in the third column under "H."

When you have finished filling in this column, divide the class into small groups and assign each group a question to research as well as a source to look into. If students can't find an answer using that source, encourage them to use other sources and list where they found the answer. Invite students to share their findings when everyone has finished.

Name _____

Date _____

KWHL

Fill in this chart before, during, and after studying a new topic.

Topic: _____

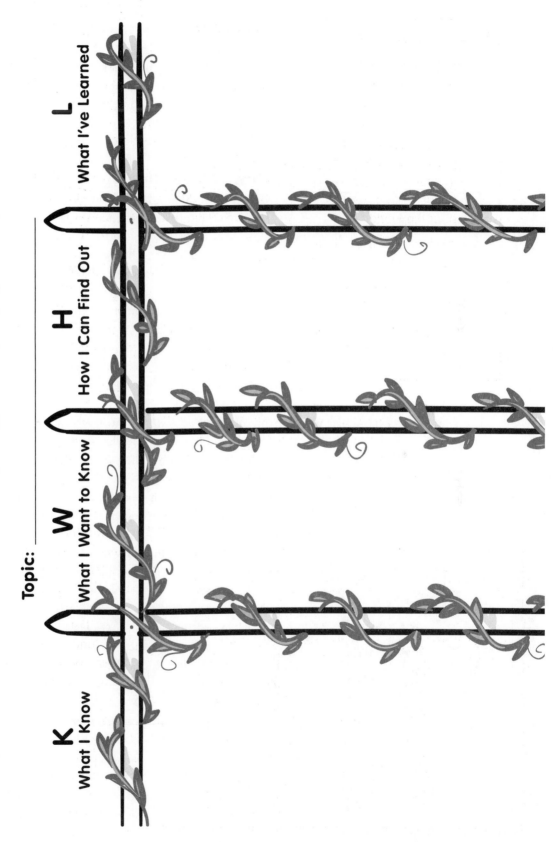

K
What I Know

W
What I Want to Know

H
How I Can Find Out

L
What I've Learned

Word Connections

Skills/Standards

- Builds science vocabulary

- Makes connections between new words and familiar words

- Explores a science concept

Purpose

Science has a language all its own with vocabulary words often not used in any other context. If students do not understand the vocabulary words in a science text, they most likely will not understand the content either. Use this graphic organizer to help students connect new science vocabulary words to more familiar words or concepts.

How to Use the Organizer

Before introducing this graphic organizer to students, select a short passage from a science textbook related to the topic you're teaching (for example, weather). Scan the passage for any words that may be unfamiliar to your students and write them on the board. Read aloud the passage to students. When you have finished, ask them if they can define any of the words on the board.

Make a transparency of the Word Connections graphic organizer (page 27) and display it on the overhead projector. At the center circle, write the topic (*weather*). Invite students to name vocabulary words related to the topic (e.g., *precipitation, evaporation, condensation*). Write the words in the circles directly connected to the center circle. Then focus on one of the words (*precipitation*) and ask students what other words they can think of that are related to this particular word (*rain, snow, sleet, hail*). If students are having a hard time coming up with related words, you may want to coach them by providing context clues. Write the related words in other circles connected to this word. (Draw additional circles, if necessary, and connect them to the word you're focusing on.) By relating the vocabulary word to more familiar words, students gain a better understanding of what the vocabulary word means.

Divide the class into pairs or small groups. Distribute copies of the graphic organizer to students and have them work together to generate related words to the other vocabulary words. Use the graphic organizer whenever studying a new topic with unfamiliar vocabulary words.

More to Do

Students can also use this organizer as a web to generate and connect ideas related to a particular topic.

Name Kendra   Date Oct. 5

Word Connections

In the center circle, write a science topic. List vocabulary words related to the topic in the connected circles.

green
wavelength
spectrum
pigment
chlorophyll
sunlight
chloroplast
Topic
photosynthesis
energy
sugar
glucose
chemical reaction
carbon dioxide
starch
energy
water

Word Connections

In the center circle, write a science topic. List vocabulary
words related to the topic in the connected circles.

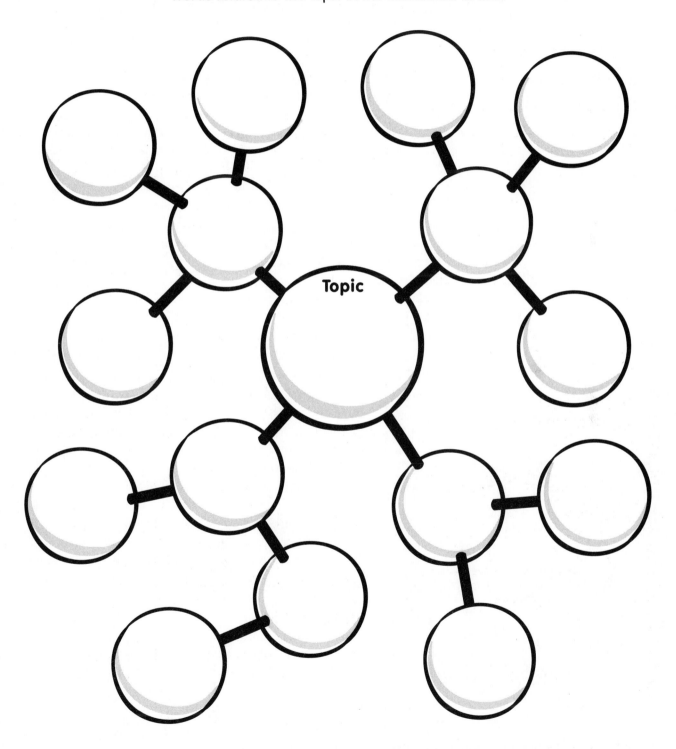

Topic

Follow the Cycle

Skills / Standards

- Understands that plants and animals progress through life cycles

- Explores the details of life cycles for different organisms

- Investigates other processes that also follow a cycle, such as the water cycle

Purpose

All life on earth follows a pattern of birth, growth and development, reproduction, and death that repeats in a never-ending life cycle. Students pick different organisms and explore the different stages of their life cycles using the graphic organizer.

How to Use the Organizer

Distribute copies of the Follow the Cycle graphic organizer (page 29) to students. Display a transparency copy on the overhead projector as well. Ask: *What is a life cycle? (A continuous process of birth, growth, reproduction, and death that all organisms go through)* Explain that a life cycle is usually represented by something that goes round and round because it's a continuous cycle that keeps repeating itself.

Write "apple tree" in the center circle and draw a picture of an apple seed on the upper right-hand corner of the graphic organizer on the overhead. Explain that the seed represents the beginning of life for a plant. As the seed germinates and gets water, food, and light, it grows into a young plant. Draw a sapling in the second section below the seed. As the plant matures into a full-grown apple tree, it produces flower blossoms. Draw a flowering apple tree in the third section. Explain that bees pollinate the flowers, which then develop seeds inside. The seeds become housed inside apple fruits that we eat. The apple tree will continue to produce flowers, seeds, and fruits for many years until it eventually dies. Draw a rotting log in the last section. Explain that even though the apple tree died, some of its seeds found their way to good growing soil and will start the whole cycle again.

Invite students to map out the life cycles of other organisms on their graphic organizers and share them with the rest of the class. Encourage students to choose different organisms, either plant or animal, so that there are no overlaps. Have students write a short description of each stage of the life cycle.

More to Do

Other process on Earth also repeat in a continuous cycle, like the water cycle. Challenge students to think of other such cycles and map them on their graphic organizers.

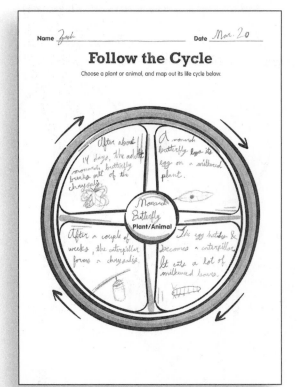

Follow the Cycle

Choose a plant or animal and map out its life cycle below.

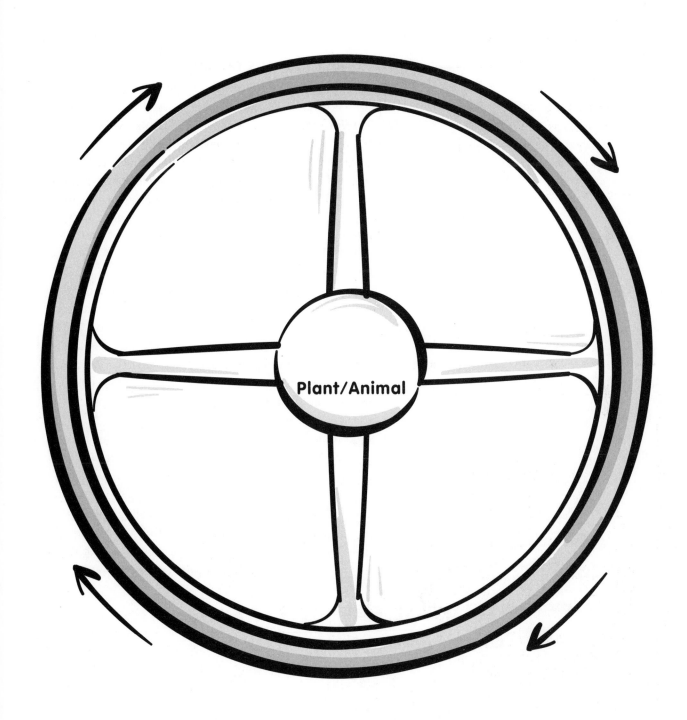

Plant/Animal

Series of Events

Skills/Standards

- Understands that many processes progress as a linear series of events

- Orders events in sequence

Purpose

Not all processes or events happen in a cycle. Some follow a linear sequence of events with an identifiable beginning and ending; for example, how a tornado forms. Using this graphic organizer, students can track the events of a particular science process and follow its sequence.

How to Use the Organizer

Have students think about something they do in which they follow a series of steps, like cooking. Using student input, outline the steps of cooking scrambled eggs, starting from when they crack the eggs' shells to when they transfer the cooked eggs from the pan to a plate. Ask: *How is this process different from something like a butterfly's life cycle, for example? (This process progresses in a linear fashion with a definite beginning and end, while a life cycle repeats again and again.)* Explain that while many processes in science follow a cycle, other processes follow a linear progression. Challenge students to think about some processes that happen linearly; for example, digestion or how a volcano forms. List their ideas on the board.

Distribute copies of the Series of Events graphic organizer (page 31) to students. Divide the class into small groups and assign each group a particular process. Have students think about what the first step might be in the process, and write it in the first box. Have them continue filling in the rest of the boxes in sequential order until they reach the end of the process. (Let students know that they may not necessarily fill in all the boxes on the graphic organizer. Likewise, if they need more space, encourage students to draw additional boxes or use a second copy of the graphic organizer.) Direct students to resources such as the Internet or textbooks for research.

When they have completed their graphic organizer, have students create a presentation based on their research.

More to Do

Students can also use this graphic organizer to outline the steps of a science experiment. See "Steps of the Scientific Method" (page 8).

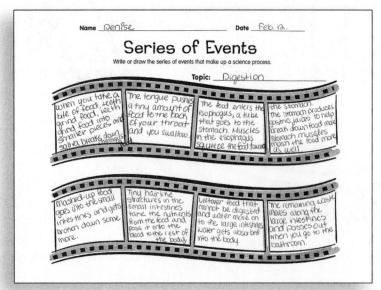

Name _____ Date _____

Series of Events

Write or draw the series of events that make up a science process.

Topic: _____

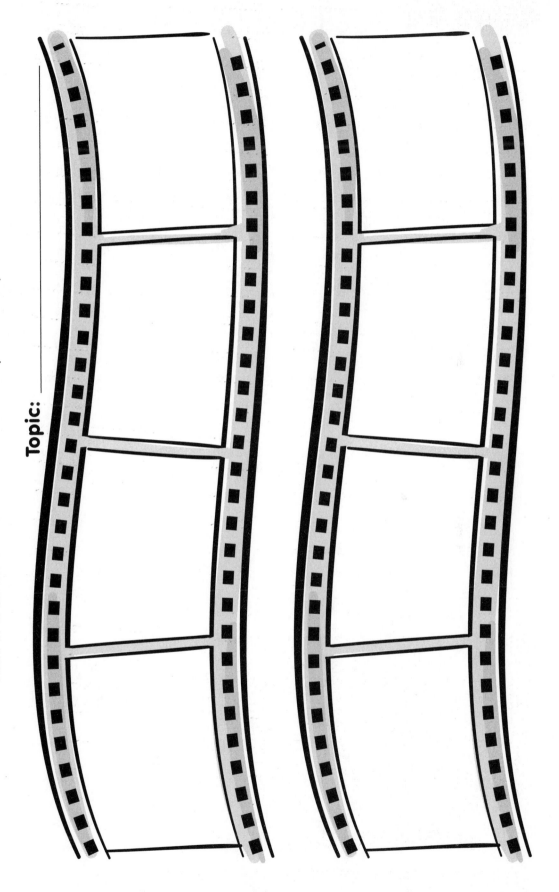

Food Chain

Skills/Standards

- Understands the organization of simple food chains

- Knows how organisms interact and depend on one another through food chains

- Explores how energy is transferred through food chains in an ecosystem

Purpose

Students will gain an understanding of what makes a food chain and explore how organisms depend on one another for food and energy.

How to Use the Organizer

Make a transparency of the Food Chain graphic organizer (page 33), and distribute photocopies to students. Ask students: *What is a food chain? (A group of interrelated organisms in which one organism feeds on a lower-level organism and is eaten by a higher-level one)* Display the transparency on the overhead projector and explain to students that you will be listing a particular food chain. Draw the sun in the first link. Ask: *Why do you think the sun is at the top of the food chain? (The sun is the original source of energy in all food chains.) What uses the sun's energy to make its own food? (Plants)* Explain that plants, including microscopic phytoplankton in the ocean, make their own food using the sun's energy through photosynthesis. Write "plants" or draw a picture of a plant on the chain link right after the sun. Next, ask: *What eats plants? (Answers will vary, but should be some type of herbivorous animal.)* Choose an appropriate answer and write it inside the next chain link. Then ask students: *What eats this animal?* Fill in the next chain link as students come up with an appropriate answer. Repeat until the rest of the food chain is filled up.

Divide the class into pairs or small groups. Have students work together to think up of other food chains and fill in their own graphic organizers. When students are finished, invite volunteers to share their food chains with the rest of the class.

More to Do

Just as humans eat more than one type of food, most animals eat a variety of foods. Have students draw additional links and fill them with other food sources for the animals on the chain to create a food web.

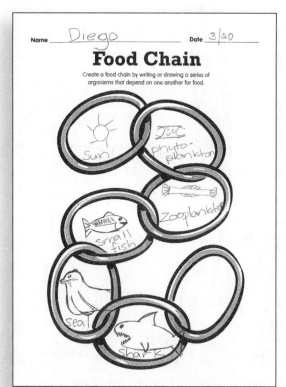

Name Diego   Date 3/20

Food Chain

Create a food chain by writing or drawing a series of organisms that depend on one another for food.

Food Chain

Create a food chain by writing or drawing a series of
organisms that depend on one another for food.

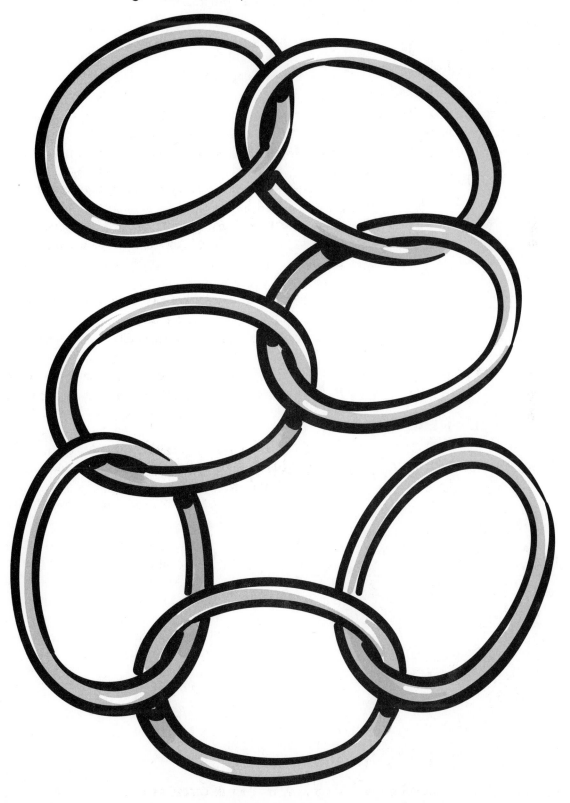

Web of Life

Skills / Standards

- Identifies characteristics of a biome or ecosystem

- Recognizes relationships among organisms and their physical environment

- Knows that an ecosystem is all populations living together and the physical factors they interact with

- Understands that all organisms, including humans, cause changes in their environment, and that these changes can be beneficial or detrimental

Purpose

The Earth consists of several *biomes*—complex communities of plants and animals that live together in particular climatic regions. Examples of land or terrestrial biomes include deserts, tundra, coniferous forests, deciduous forests, rainforests, and grasslands. Aquatic biomes include oceans, ponds, rivers, and lakes. By studying the different biomes in our world, students will understand that we share this planet with numerous unique species and that we need to help preserve their homes if we are to save them from extinction.

How to Use the Organizer

Ask students: *What is a biome? (A community of plants and animals living together in a particular climate and region)* Explain to students that the desert is an example of a biome. If possible, display a world map and ask students to point out and name the location of some deserts; for example, the Sahara desert in northern Africa, the Gobi desert in Asia, and the Sonoran desert in the United States. Ask: *What are some characteristics of a desert? (Dry, hot, little rainfall, few plants and animals)* Explain to students that the Earth is made up of other biomes, such as rainforest, deciduous forest, tundra, and grassland, and that each biome has its own characteristics and community of plants and animals that live there.

Divide the class into five or six groups and assign each group a biome to research. Distribute copies of the Web of Life graphic organizer (page 35) to students. Have students conduct research to find out characteristics of their assigned biome, where it's located, and what the climate is like. They should also provide examples of plants and animals that live there, including how they have adapted to this particular biome. Finally, have students find out how humans have impacted this biome and what we can do to help preserve it. When they have completed their research, encourage each group to create a presentation about their biome and share the information with the class.

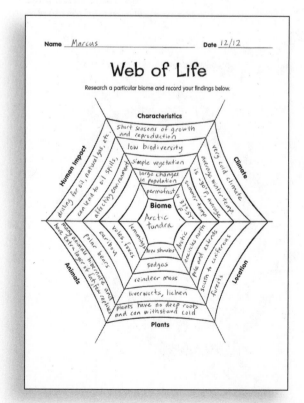

Web of Life

Research a particular biome and record your findings below.

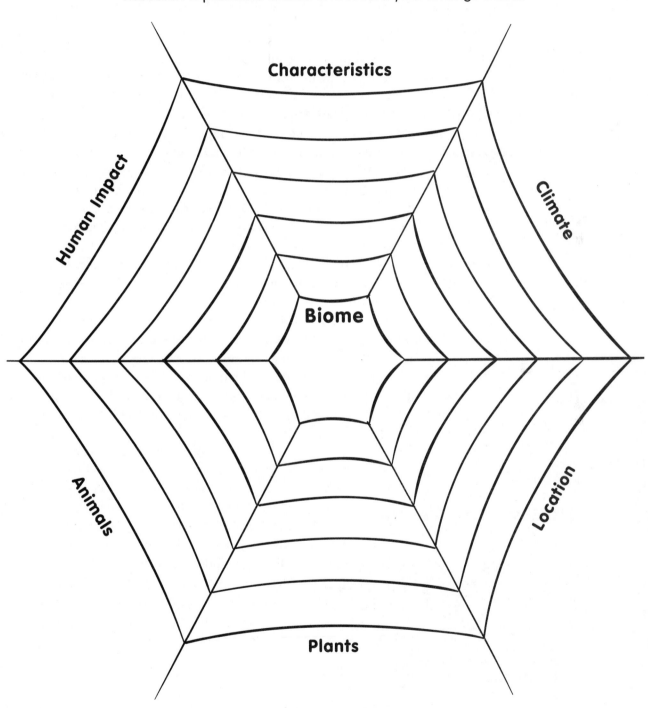

Characteristics

Human Impact

Climate

Biome

Animals

Location

Plants

Parts of a Whole

Skills/Standards

- Understands the structure and properties of matter

- Identifies the composition of different types of matter

Purpose

Everything in this universe is a form of matter. At the most basic level, matter consists of tiny particles called *atoms* that link together in different ways to form wide varieties of structures, from microscopic molecules to superclusters of galaxies. Students will enjoy exploring these different structures and finding out what they are composed of using this graphic organizer.

How to Use the Organizer

Make a transparency of the Parts of a Whole graphic organizer (page 37) and display it on the overhead projector. Ask students to describe the image on the organizer. *(A beam of light passing through a prism and being separated into different bands of color)* Explain to students that just as white light is composed of the different wavelengths, or colors, of light, other matters in science are composed of other things as well. The Earth's atmosphere, for example, is made up of a variety of gases.

On the transparency, write *atmosphere* on the left side of the prism. Ask students: *What are some of the gases that make up our atmosphere? (Nitrogen, oxygen, carbon dioxide, water vapor, argon, and trace amounts of other gases)* As students name the correct gases, write each one on a band to the right of the prism. Explain to students that another way to "break down" the atmosphere is by its layers: *troposphere, stratosphere, mesosphere, thermosphere,* and *exosphere.* (Let students know that it's okay if they don't fill up all the bands.) Distribute copies of the graphic organizer to students and have them conduct research on the different layers of the atmosphere, and write a short description of each layer on each band.

Encourage students to look for other things they can break down into components, such as the ocean, computers, electromagnetic radiation (the invisible spectrum), simple machines, and so on.

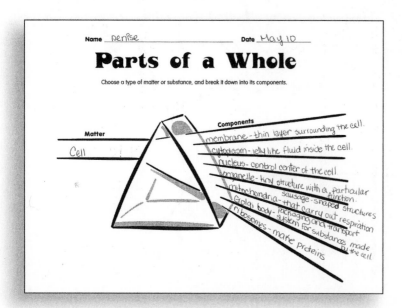

Name Denise   Date May 10

Parts of a Whole

Choose a type of matter or substance, and break it down into its components.

Matter

Cell

Components

membrane - thin layer surrounding the cell.

cytoplasm - jelly like fluid inside the cell.

nucleus - control center of the cell

organelle - tiny structure with a particular function.

mitochondria - sausage-shaped structures that carry out respiration

Golgi body - packaging and transport system for substances made by the cell

ribosomes - make proteins

Name —————

Date —————

Parts of a Whole

Choose a type of matter or substance and break it down into its components.

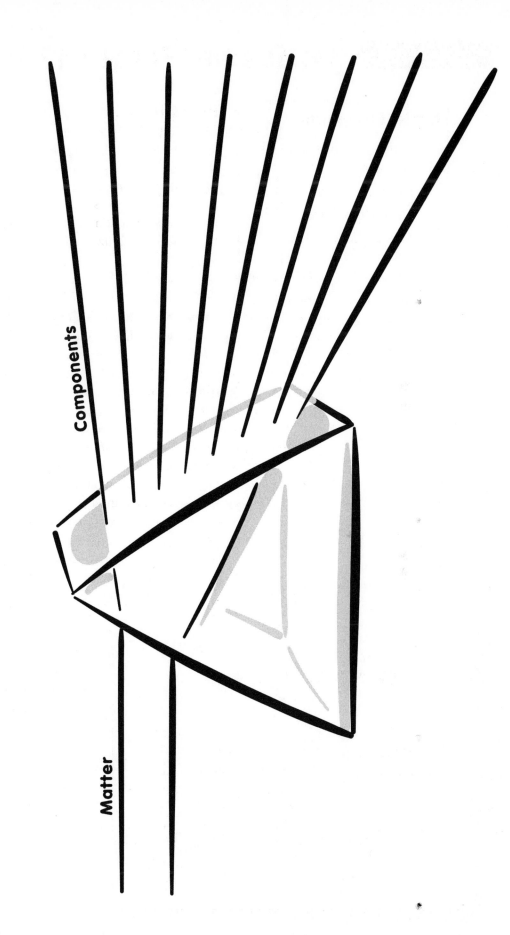

Components

Matter

What's the Solution?

Skills/Standards

- Explores mixtures and solutions

- Investigates how substances react chemically with other substances to form new substances

- Understands relationships in science formulas

Purpose

In physical science, a *solution* is a homogenous mixture formed when a solid, liquid, or gas is combined with another solid, liquid, or gas. The most basic use of this graphic organizer is to identify a *solute* (substance that is dissolved to form a solution) and a *solvent* (substance that is used to dissolve other substances) then describe the resulting solution. Students can also use this graphic organizer to describe the chemical reaction that occurs when two or more chemicals are mixed together.

How to Use the Organizer

Demonstrate this simple experiment to introduce the graphic organizer: Put about a teaspoon of baking soda into one beaker and some vinegar in a separate beaker. Display a transparency of the What's the Solution? graphic organizer (page 39) on the overhead projector, writing *vinegar* in one test tube and *baking soda* in the other.

Ask students: *What do you think will happen when I pour this vinegar into the baking soda? (The solution will bubble up and eventually overflow.)* Carefully pour the vinegar into the first beaker, encouraging students to observe what happens. Call on a volunteer to write or draw on the transparency what he or she observed. Explain to students that vinegar is an acid, whereas baking soda is a base. When the two ingredients combine, the acid neutralizes the base, releasing carbon dioxide and creating the bubbling that they see—a chemical reaction. Have students use this graphic organizer when they're conducting experiments with solutions or chemical reactions.

Students can also use this graphic organizer to show relationships in science. For example, consider the formula $F = ma$ (force = mass × acceleration). Have students use the graphic organizer to describe the relationship between mass and acceleration to produce force, or to show other science formulas.

More to Do

You can also extend this graphic organizer to math word problems to help students visualize numbers in equations. Simply add an operation sign to describe the relationship between two numbers (students can draw additional "test tubes" to work with more numbers) and record the solution in the beaker.

Name ___Diego___ Date __10/5__

What's the Solution?

Use this graphic organizer to record what happens when two (or more) substances combine.

1 atom of carbon

Substance

2 atoms of oxygen

Substance

CO_2
carbon dioxide
a colorless, odorless gas that is present in the air

Solution

What's the Solution?

Use this graphic organizer to record what happens
when two (or more) substances combine.

Substance

Substance

Solution

On a Scale

Skills/Standards

- Understands how measurement tools are used to gather, analyze, and interpret data

- Explores the different scales of measurement used in science

Purpose

Scientists use different scales to measure wind speed, earthquake intensity, the hardness of minerals, and more. Encourage students to investigate and learn more about various scales used in science with this graphic organizer.

How to Use the Organizer

Engage students in a discussion about the tools we use for measuring and what we measure with them. For example, we use thermometers to measure temperature, metersticks to measure length, speedometers to measure speed, and so on. Explain that measurement is an essential aspect of science. Scientists measure the size of atoms and galaxies, the temperature at the center of the sun and of deep space, the speed of light, and so on.

Sometimes scientists measure things on a scale. Explain that the word *scale* in this case does not mean the tool used for measuring weight. Rather, it means a series of marks or points set at regular intervals to measure something. For example, the Richter magnitude scale measures the strength of an earthquake. An earthquake with a magnitude 2.0 or less is usually not felt by people, while earthquakes of magnitude 4.5 and above are often detectable.

Encourage students to investigate various scales used in science, such as the Richter scale, the Mohs hardness scale, the Beaufort wind scale, the Fujita tornado scale, and more. You can either assign a scale to groups of students or let students choose a scale to learn more about.

Distribute copies of the On a Scale graphic organizer (page 41) to students. Have them record the levels of the scale (from lowest to highest, or vice-versa) on the piano keys and describe each level's characteristics on the line next to the appropriate key. For example, in the Fujita scale, F0 is a light tornado with wind speeds of 40 to 72 miles per hour; tree branches are broken, and chimneys and large signs are damaged.

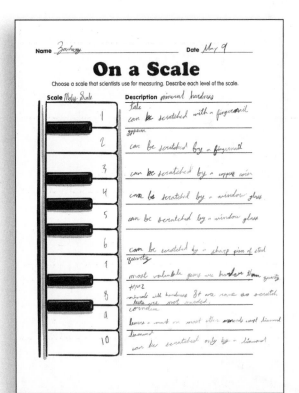

Name _____   **Date** _____

On a Scale

Choose a scale that scientists use for measuring. Describe each level of the scale.

Scale

Description

Time Vine

Skills / Standards

- Understands the scientific enterprise

- Knows that people of all ages, backgrounds, and groups have made contributions to science and technology throughout history

- Recognizes that although people using scientific inquiry have learned much about the objects, events, and phenomena in nature, science is an ongoing process and will never be finished

Purpose

Science is an evolving study. The earliest people made discoveries in science (e.g., how to produce and control fire), and throughout history many more individuals have made valuable discoveries and contributions that have helped shape our scientific knowledge today. Learning about the history of science, including the people who were involved, helps students gain a better understanding of scientific inquiry and the role science plays in our society.

How to Use the Organizer

Engage students in a discussion about how science has evolved over time. For example, in ancient Greece, Aristotle and Ptolemy believed that the Earth was at the center of the universe and everything else revolved around our planet. Then in the 16th century, Copernicus forwarded a revolutionary idea that placed the sun at the center of the universe. Later, Johannes Kepler formulated the laws of planetary motion, showing that the sun is at the center of our solar system and that the planets revolve around the sun in elliptical orbits. Other scientists made their own discoveries and contributions over time, and today we know that our sun is an ordinary star that is merely one of innumerable stars in the universe.

Explain to students that every field of science has its own history of contributions and discoveries that have led to what we know today. Studying the history of science is important in learning how the scientific process works and how ideas evolve over time. Distribute copies of the Time Vine graphic organizer (page 43) to students. Encourage students to pick a particular field that they would like to study and conduct research on important events that have happened in that field. Have students write the topic or field above the vine, then write the dates and events on each leaf in order, from top to bottom. Let students add more leaves or use a second copy of the graphic organizer if necessary.

More to Do

Have students use this organizer when researching the life of a scientist, noting important dates and events in that scientist's life on the leaves.

Time Vine

Research and record important dates and events in the history of science.

Topic: _____

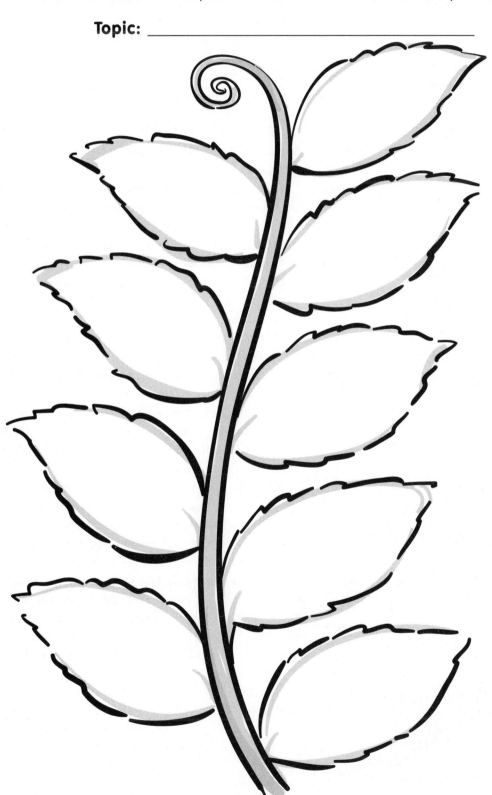

Balancing Issues

Skills/Standards

- Understands ethics associated with scientific study

- Knows ways in which science and society influence one another

- Identifies controversial issues in science

- Conducts research to learn both sides of an issue

- Develops critical-thinking skills

Purpose

Science may be a study in search of facts, but that doesn't keep it from having its share of controversy. Many people feel very strongly about certain science-related issues, such as animal testing or human exploration of space. Using this graphic organizer, students will conduct research on a controversial topic and list arguments for both sides of the topic, then decide which side they support.

How to Use the Organizer

Ask students: *What do you know about animal testing?* Explain that some companies use lab animals, such as mice and rats, to test various products ranging from cosmetics to household cleaners to cancer medicines. People have very different views about this topic—some are for animal testing and some are against it. Divide the class into two groups. Assign one group to be *for* animal testing and the other group *against* animal testing. Give students up to 10 minutes to discuss and build up a case for their side.

Make a transparency of the Balancing Issues graphic organizer (page 45) and display it on the overhead projector. On the scale's base, write "Animal Testing." Then alternately call on volunteers from each side to give a reason for (or against) animal testing. Record reasons for animal testing on one side of the scale, and reasons against it on the other side. You may want to invite students to discuss the issue further, but try to discourage animosity by explaining that in controversial issues such as this, it's never easy to tell which side is correct. This is why it's important to conduct thorough research on both sides of the issue before deciding which side you support.

If possible, list other controversial science-related issues on the board, such as genetic engineering, use of nuclear energy, or teaching evolution in the classroom. (Make sure the topics are appropriate to your students.) You may want to put students into small groups and assign an issue to each group. Distribute copies of the graphic organizer for students to use in their research.

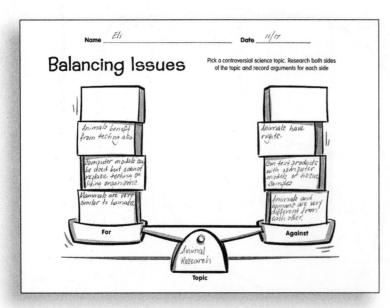

Name _____

Balancing Issues

Pick a controversial science topic. Research both sides
of the topic and record arguments for each side.

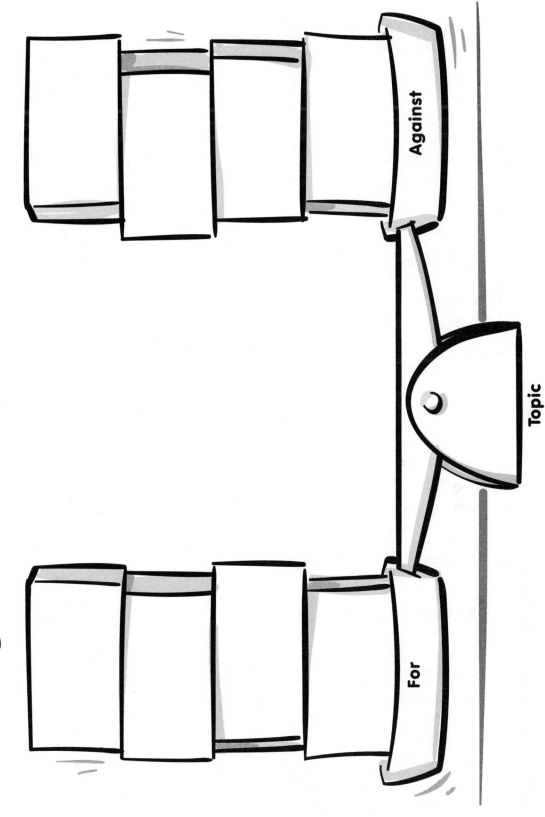

For

Against

Topic

Careers in Science

Skills/Standards

- Explores careers in science

- Knows that people of all ages, backgrounds, and groups have made contributions to science and technology throughout history

- Understands that the work of science requires a variety of human abilities, qualities, and habits of mind

- Identifies various settings in which scientists and engineers may work

Purpose

Science is such a large field of study that one scientist is likely to be doing something completely different from another scientist. This graphic organizer will help students explore various fields of science and the careers that they can offer.

How to Use the Organizer

Ask students: *What is a scientist? What are some things that a scientist might do or study?* Students may be surprised to know that there are many different kinds of scientists, like astronomers, biologists, chemists, zoologists, and more. But within each of these fields, scientists can specialize even further. For example, some astronomers search for life on other planets, while others focus on how the universe formed. Some help plan space missions, while others conduct experiments in space.

Invite students to explore different careers in science. Distribute copies of the Careers in Science graphic organizer (page 47) and have students use it to learn more about a particular career in science. You may want to provide a preliminary list of careers, such as those listed above. You can either assign each student a career or let students pick which one they would like to research. Encourage students to use the list as a springboard and try to narrow down the fields to more specialized careers. For example, instead of researching biologists, a student might research marine biologists or biotechnologists. To avoid repeats, ask students to let you know what career they've chosen before they start their research.

The Internet offers a wealth of Web sites on science careers. You may want to direct students to a search engine, such as Google, and type in "careers in science" or "science careers." Have students find out what level of education is required, including what subjects to take, where this type of scientist might work (e.g., on the field or for the military), what kind of work the scientist does, and what other specialties this career might offer. Let students know that finding all the information in the graphic organizer may be challenging, but they should try their best.

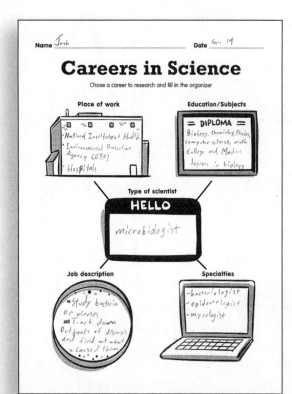

Careers in Science

Choose a career to research and fill in the organizer.

Workplace

Education/Subjects

= DIPLOMA =

Type of scientist

HELLO

Job description

Specialties

Bibliography

Bromley, K., L. Irwin-De Vitis, & M. Modlo. (1995). *Graphic Organizers: Visual Strategies for Active Learning.* New York: Scholastic Inc.

Boyle, J.R. & M. Weishaar. (1997). "The Effects of Expert-Generated Versus Student-Generated Cognitive Organizers on the Reading Comprehension of Students with Learning Disabilities." *Learning Disabilities Research and Practice*, 12(4), 228–235.

Chang, K.E., Y.T. Sung, & I.D. Chen. (2002). "The Effect of Concept Mapping to Enhance Text Comprehension and Summarization." *Journal of Experimental Education*, 71(1), 5–24.

Dodge, J. (2005). *Differentiation in Action.* New York: Scholastic Inc.

Ellis, E.S. (1994). "Integrating Writing Instruction with Content-Area Instruction: Part II: Writing Processes." *Intervention in School and Clinic*, 29(4), 219–230.

Guastello, E.F. (2000). "Concept Mapping Effects on Science Content Comprehension of Low-Achieving Inner-City Seventh Graders." *Remedial and Special Education*, 21(6), 356.

Moore, D. & J. Readence. (1984). "A Quantitative and Qualitative Review of Graphic Organizer Research." *Journal of Educational Research*, 78(1), 11–17.

National Center on Accessing the General Curriculum. (2002). http://www.cast.org/index.html